Sell Yourself

Lucie Dupont

Lucie Dupont

Copyright Page

Index

Lucie Dupont

The Power of Personal Branding

The power of personal branding is something we all have, even without realizing it. From the moment we interact with other people, we are already projecting an image of who we are, what values we have, and what we can offer. Personal branding is not just for celebrities or big businessmen; it is something that anyone can build, and it is essential if you want to stand out in any area of your life, whether professional or personal.

Imagine that every time someone mentions you, they do so based on a clear idea of who you are and what you stand for. That's your brand. Every word you say, every post you make on social media, every conversation you have, everything contributes to building that perception that others have of you. In a world as competitive as today's, where there are thousands of people looking for the same opportunities, a strong personal brand can be the decisive factor that makes you stand out. But it's not just about being different, it's about being authentic and consistent with who you really are.

One of the biggest advantages of having a recognized personal brand is that it opens doors. People trust brands they know and respect, and if you can position yourself as someone trustworthy, opportunities will start to come without you having to actively seek them out. You will become a reference, someone people turn to for advice, work, or collaboration. But to get to that point, it is essential that you know yourself and know what you have to offer. A strong personal brand is not based on pretending to be someone you are not, but on highlighting your genuine qualities and making those qualities visible to others.

Plus, a personal brand allows you to control the narrative about who you are. Instead of letting others decide what they think about you, you define that perception. You choose what aspects of your life or career to show, what story to tell, and how to present yourself to the world. And while it may seem superficial, the reality is that a good personal brand has a profound impact on how you feel about yourself. It gives you confidence, makes you feel more secure in presenting yourself to others, and allows you to connect in a more authentic and effective way with your audience, whether they are clients, colleagues, or friends.

The power of personal branding also lies in longevity. Trends pass, companies change, but a strong personal brand can last a lifetime. If you work on it constantly, adapting it to changes in your life and in the world, you can stay relevant no matter what happens around you. And that's one of the biggest advantages of investing time and effort into building a personal brand. It's a long-term investment, one that will continue to pay off, even when you decide to change careers or direction.

But not everything is positive if you don't know how to manage your brand well. As with any kind of reputation, it can be fragile. One wrong move, a lack of coherence in what you say or do, can jeopardize everything you've built. That's why personal branding requires constant care and attention. It's not something you can build overnight and then forget about. You have to nurture it, be aware of how you present yourself and what message you're sending, both in the physical and digital world.

In short, personal branding is a powerful tool that, if used correctly, can open many doors and improve your life both professionally and personally. It's not about inventing a character or pretending to be someone you're not, but about identifying your strengths and values and showing them authentically and consistently to the world. We all have a personal brand, whether we know it or not. The question is whether we're going to take control of it or let others define it for us. And once you decide to take control of your own brand, the power you have to influence how others perceive you is immense.

Self-knowledge

Self-awareness is the starting point of any strong personal brand. Before you can present yourself to the world authentically and effectively, it's essential to know yourself. It seems obvious, but many people go through life without taking the time to reflect on who they really are, what they want, and what they have to offer. If you don't know who you are, how are you going to build a brand that genuinely represents you?

Knowing yourself involves understanding your strengths and weaknesses, recognizing your values and principles, and being clear about your goals in life. It is a deep introspection that goes beyond what you do on a day-to-day basis or what others see of you. It is asking yourself what moves you, what you are passionate about, what makes you different from others, and how you can use those aspects to stand out. All of this requires honesty, because it is easy to fall into the trap of wanting to be someone we are not or projecting an image that we believe others expect to see.

The first step to self-awareness is accepting that we're not perfect, and that's okay. We all have strengths, but also areas in which we need to improve. Identifying what those strengths are will help you build an authentic personal brand, based on what really makes you special. Maybe you're very creative, or maybe you have an innate ability to solve problems. Maybe your greatest strength is that you're a good listener. Whatever it is, it's important to discover and acknowledge it, because it will be the foundation of your brand.

But it's not just about identifying what you do well. Knowing yourself also means being aware of your weaknesses. We all have aspects that we don't master or that we find more difficult, and being honest with yourself about these points will not only help you work on them, but will also make you more human and accessible. People like to connect with real people, not perfect images. So don't be afraid to acknowledge your limitations, because that's also part of what makes you unique.

In addition to your strengths and weaknesses, self-awareness also involves reflecting on your values. What really matters to you? What principles guide your life? Maybe you value honesty above all else, or perhaps your focus is on creativity and innovation. These values not only define you as a person, but they also influence how you present yourself to the world. If your personal brand is not aligned with your values, sooner or later the lack of coherence will become noticeable, and that can negatively affect how others perceive you.

An important part of self-awareness is also understanding your goals. What do you want to achieve in the long term? Where do you see yourself in five or ten years? Having a clear vision of your goals will allow you to focus your personal brand in the right direction. If you are not clear about where you want to go, it will be difficult to build a brand that will take you there. And it's not just about professional goals; it's also important to think about your personal goals. Sometimes, our personal and professional success are more connected than we think, and a well-built personal brand should reflect that balance.

Self-knowledge is not something that is achieved overnight. It is an ongoing process that requires time and reflection. People change, they evolve, and the same goes for our personal brands. What is important to you today may not be important in a few years. That is why it is essential that you take the time to constantly review and adjust how you feel about yourself and your brand. The idea is for both to be in sync, and to do that you need to spend time getting to know yourself thoroughly.

Self-awareness not only helps you build a more authentic personal brand, but it also gives you the confidence to present yourself to others without fear of judgment or criticism. When you know who you are and what you can bring to the table, you become more confident in your interactions, and that is reflected in the way others perceive you. It's not about being arrogant, but about knowing that you're being true to yourself, and that's one of the best foundations on which to build a strong, lasting brand.

In short, self-awareness is the cornerstone of any personal brand. You can't begin to build a coherent public image if you're not clear about who you really are. Knowing yourself will allow you to highlight your strengths, work on your weaknesses, align your brand with your values, and define your long-term goals. Most importantly, it will give you the confidence to be authentic in everything you do. If you achieve this, your personal brand will be much more than just an image; it will be a faithful and powerful representation of who you really are.

Defining your Unique Value Proposition (UVP)

Defining your Unique Value Proposition, also known as UVP, is one of the most important steps in building a strong personal brand. Simply put, your UVP is what makes you different from everyone else, what sets you apart and makes you the best option in your field. It's what makes you valuable and unique, and what will make people choose you over someone else.

Think of your VSP as the heart of your personal brand. While many may have similar skills to you or work in the same field, only you have a unique combination of qualities, experiences, and perspectives that set you apart. Defining that value proposition is essential to being able to clearly communicate why you are special and why people should trust you. It's not about being better than others, but about showing what makes you unique and how you can offer something that others can't.

The first step in defining your UVP is to reflect on your strengths and what makes you stand out. What are you really good at? What types of problems can you solve better than others? Here it is important to be honest with yourself and identify what truly sets you apart. It may be a technical skill, such as being very efficient at solving complex problems, or it may be something more related to your personal qualities, such as having a great ability to connect emotionally with people. There is no right answer, but the essential thing is to identify those qualities that really make you stand out.

Another key aspect in defining your UVP is to consider your audience or target audience. You can't just focus on what you think makes you unique; you also need to think about what your audience needs and values. What are they looking for? What kind of problems do they have, and how can you help them solve them? If you manage to align what makes you unique with what your audience is looking for, you'll have taken a huge step in building a powerful UVP. In other words, your UVP is not just about you, but about how your skills and qualities can bring value to others.

A good example of a UVP would be to think of someone who works as a personal trainer. There are many trainers in the world, but perhaps this particular one specializes in helping people with busy schedules stay fit through short but effective workout routines. Your UVP wouldn't simply be "I'm a good trainer," but something more specific like "I help busy people get fit with efficient workouts that fit into their busy day." This type of value proposition is clear, direct, and speaks directly to a specific audience, highlighting what makes you different from other trainers.

Once you've identified what makes you unique and how that can benefit others, the next step is being able to communicate it clearly and concisely. Often, people know what makes them special, but they don't know how to explain it. This is where the skill of distilling your UVP into a sentence or two that are easy to understand and that summarise exactly what you offer comes into play. This is the sentence you will use in your pitch when you introduce yourself to others, whether in an interview, a business meeting or on your social media. It should be clear, direct and show the value you bring to the table.

A common mistake made when defining your UVP is trying to cover too much or be too general. The key is to be specific. If you try to be everything to everyone, you'll end up being nothing to anyone. Instead of trying to cover too many bases, focus on one or two areas where you really shine and that set you apart from others. Don't be afraid to be specific, because the clearer you are about what you offer, the easier it will be for the right people to connect with you.

The UVP should also be consistent with who you are and your values. There's no point in defining a value proposition that doesn't align with what you can actually offer or what you care about. If your UVP is disconnected from your true essence, people will quickly notice, and it will negatively impact your credibility. Authenticity is key here. Make sure that what you promise in your UVP is something you can deliver and that it truly reflects who you are and what you stand for.

Finally, it's important to remember that your UVP isn't something fixed and immutable. Over time, as you grow professionally and personally, your value proposition can change and evolve. What makes you unique today might not be the same in five or ten years, and that's okay. The key is to revisit your UVP periodically and make sure it remains relevant and authentic. This way, your personal brand will always stay fresh and aligned with who you are at every stage of your life.

In short, your Unique Value Proposition is what sets you apart from others and what makes people choose you over others. Defining it requires honest introspection, a deep understanding of what your customers or audience value, and the ability to communicate it clearly and concisely. It is a powerful tool that, if used correctly, can open many doors and help you build a strong and authentic personal brand. So take the time to define it well, because it will be the foundation on which your entire personal brand will be built.

Building Your Personal Story

Building your personal story is one of the most important aspects when it comes to creating a strong personal brand. We all love stories, because they connect us, allow us to understand people, and make us feel something. Your personal story is the way you communicate who you are, where you come from, what you have lived through, and how those experiences have led you to be who you are today. It is a powerful tool, because through it you can show your authenticity, highlight what makes you unique, and create an emotional connection with those who listen to you or follow you.

Often, when we think about telling our story, we are tempted to only talk about our accomplishments or how well we have done in certain aspects. But what really connects with people is not a list of successes, but the authenticity and difficulties you have overcome. Everyone has challenges in life, difficult moments, and it is those experiences that make your story human and relatable. People connect more easily when they see that you have been through similar situations to those they have experienced or when they can understand your emotions and challenges.

To begin building your personal story, it's helpful to think about key moments in your life. What events have been defining for you? Maybe it was a major career change, a difficult decision you made, or an experience that changed your way of seeing the world. These moments are what form the basis of your story and will help you show your human side, that part of you that makes you more approachable and genuine.

You don't have to include every detail of your life in your personal story. In fact, less is more. The idea is not to tell your entire life story, but to choose the moments and experiences that best reflect who you are and what defines you. Maybe there was a big obstacle you had to overcome or a failure that taught you a valuable lesson. These are the moments that will make your story memorable and allow people to see how you've grown and evolved over time. In the end, it's not just what you've experienced, but how those events have shaped the way you see things and act.

It's important that your personal story aligns with the unique value proposition you've defined. It's not just about telling anecdotes, but about showing how those experiences reinforce what you offer. If your UVP is that you're someone who helps others overcome the fear of failure, then your story should include moments when you yourself have faced failure and how you overcame it. This way, your story will not only be personal, but also relevant to those who listen to you or follow you, as it will show that your experience backs up what you promise.

A good example of an effective personal story is one that follows a transformation narrative. People love stories of change, because they show growth and resilience. Maybe you started out in a difficult situation, with few opportunities, but through effort, dedication, and a few lessons learned along the way, you managed to become who you are today. These types of stories not only inspire, but they also show that it is possible to overcome difficulties. And when your audience sees that in you, they may also start to believe that they can do the same in their own lives.

Another important aspect of telling your story is being authentic. Authenticity is key when building a personal brand, because people have a radar for what is fake or exaggerated. Don't try to paint a perfect picture of yourself. Accept that, like any human being, you have made mistakes, had doubts, and gone through difficult times. These are the elements that will make your story believable and authentic. People connect more with imperfections than with an idealized image.

Your personal story should also evolve over time. As you continue to grow and experience new things, your story will change. Don't be afraid to adjust or add new experiences that reflect your changes. Maybe, in the beginning, your story focused on how you found your passion for what you do. But, over time, that story might evolve to include new goals or accomplishments that have led you down a different path. The key is to keep your story alive and adapt it to each new stage of your life.

Once you've built your personal story, it's critical to know how to tell it effectively. It's not just about the facts, but how you present them. Practice telling your story in a way that flows naturally and resonates with the people you're speaking to. Use simple, clear language, and avoid overloading it with unnecessary details. You want your story to be easy to understand, engage people, and leave a lasting impression.

When telling your personal story, be sure to include emotions. Don't just describe what happened; talk about how you felt at that moment. Emotions are what really connect with people. If you felt frustrated, lost, or excited at some point in your story, don't hesitate to share it. Those emotions are what will make your story come alive and make people relate to what you're telling.

In short, building your personal story is a key process in creating a strong personal brand. It's not just about narrating what you've experienced, but about choosing the most important moments that reflect who you are and how you got to where you are today. Your story should be authentic, relevant and emotional, because it's through it that you'll be able to connect more deeply with others. And remember, a good personal story isn't static; it keeps growing with you, changing and adapting as you do too.

Visual Identity and Online Presence

Your visual identity and online presence are critical components in creating a strong personal brand. While your story and unique value proposition communicate who you are and what you offer, your visual identity is what first captures attention. It's how you visually present yourself to the world and what people remember about you when they encounter you online. In such a competitive digital environment, a consistent and engaging visual identity is key to standing out and building an instant connection with your audience.

Visual identity includes all the graphic elements that make up your personal brand: colors, fonts, logo (if you choose to have one), images, and the overall design of your online platforms. These elements work together to create a recognizable and coherent image that reflects your personality and what you stand for. It's not just about choosing a nice color or font, but about making sure that everything you display visually is aligned with the essence of your brand and the message you want to convey.

One of the first steps in building your visual identity is choosing a color palette that represents you. Colors have a huge impact on how people perceive your brand. For example, warm colors like red or orange often convey energy, passion, or urgency, while cooler hues like blue or green communicate calm, professionalism, or confidence. Think about what you want people to feel when they interact with your brand and choose colors that reinforce that feeling. It's also important to stay consistent in your use of those colors across all of your platforms so that, over time, people will associate those colors with you.

Another crucial aspect is typography. The fonts you use should be easy to read, but they should also reflect your style. If your brand is more professional and serious, you'll probably want to stick to elegant and traditional fonts. If, on the other hand, you want to convey a more relaxed or creative image, you can choose more casual or modern fonts. As with colors, it's important to be consistent in your use of fonts across all your platforms. Repetition of certain visual elements helps make your brand more recognizable and reinforces your identity.

Your logo design is another key element, although it's not always mandatory to have one. A logo can be as simple as your name written in a specific font or as complex as a symbol or image that represents what you do. The important thing is that it's something that easily identifies you and reflects your personality. You don't need a complicated logo, in fact, many of the most successful brands have simple logos that are easy to remember. If you decide to have a logo, make sure it works well in different formats, from a social media profile to a business card.

Once you've defined your visual identity, it's time to bring it to your online presence. This is where your brand really comes to life, as it's in the digital world that many people will first encounter you. The way you present yourself on your social media, website, or any other online platform should be consistent with your visual identity. This doesn't mean you have to be rigid or repetitive, but you do need to maintain a consistent line so that people can immediately recognize your brand, no matter where they find you.

Your online presence starts with the platforms you choose to be on. You don't need to be on every social network; the important thing is to be on the platforms where your audience is. If your audience is younger, platforms like Instagram or TikTok may be more relevant. If your audience is more professional, LinkedIn may be a good space to focus on. The key is to choose the platforms that allow you to effectively connect with the people you want to reach, and then tailor your visual identity and content to each of them.

Your social media profile is like your digital business card. Make sure your profile photos, cover images, and any other graphic elements reflect your visual identity. Use the colors, fonts, and visual style you've defined to create consistency across everything you do. This helps create a strong, professional image and makes it easier for people to remember you. Additionally, your bio and descriptions should align with your unique value proposition, so people immediately know who you are and what you offer.

The content you share online is also an important part of your online presence. This is where your authenticity comes into play, and how you use your visual identity to support the message you want to convey. If you share visual content, such as photos or videos, make sure they are well-designed and consistent with your style. If you prefer to share written content, such as articles or reflections, use your visual identity to highlight that content and give it a personal touch. In the end, everything you post should be aligned with your brand and provide value to your audience.

It's not just about what you share, but also how you interact with others. Your online presence also includes how you respond to comments, how you communicate with your audience, and how you participate in the online community. Your tone of voice, both in your posts and in your interactions, should be consistent with your brand. If your identity is more professional, you'll likely use a more formal tone. If, on the other hand, your brand is more approachable or relaxed, you may opt for a more conversational tone. The important thing is that whatever tone you choose, it's consistent across all your interactions.

A key aspect of online presence is consistency. It's not just about being active one day and then disappearing for weeks. To build a strong personal brand, you need to be consistent in your online activity. This doesn't mean you should post every day, but you do need to have a regular presence to keep your audience engaged and interested. Additionally, consistency in the use of your visual identity also reinforces your brand, making it easier for people to identify you over time.

In short, your visual identity and online presence are essential to creating a recognizable and effective personal brand. Your visual identity helps you capture people's attention and convey a consistent message about who you are and what you stand for. Your online presence is the platform where that identity comes to life and connects with your audience. By ensuring that both aspects are aligned and consistent, you'll be building a strong, memorable and authentic brand that will help you stand out in the digital world.

Creating Strategic Relationships

Building strategic relationships is one of the most powerful steps to strengthening your personal brand and effectively growing it. While having skills and knowledge is important, many times what really drives your success is the people you connect with. Strategic relationships are those connections that not only bring you value, but also allow you to create opportunities for mutual growth. These relationships aren't built overnight, but with dedication and authenticity, you can create a network that helps you achieve your goals while supporting others in their pursuits.

The first step in creating strategic relationships is to identify people who can have a positive impact on your professional or personal development. This doesn't mean that you should only seek relationships with influential or successful people. Instead, you should look for people who share your interests, values, and who are in fields related to yours. These connections can be with colleagues in your industry, mentors, clients, or even with people who are just starting out in your field but show potential. The important thing is to build a network of people who complement each other and can support each other.

Once you've identified the people you'd like to connect with, the next step is to genuinely approach them. The key here is to build relationships based on mutual interest, not convenience. Sometimes when we think about strategic relationships, we're tempted to approach someone just because we think they can help us accomplish something, but that approach rarely works in the long run. The best strategic relationships are built when both parties feel they can bring something valuable to the other. So before you ask for something, think about how you can be helpful to that person. It might be by offering an interesting perspective, helping them with a problem, or simply sharing valuable resources.

Authenticity is key when it comes to building relationships. People can tell when someone is approaching you with superficial intentions or purely out of self-interest. For a strategic relationship to really work, there must be a genuine interest in the other person, what they do, and how you both can benefit from that connection. This means you must be willing to invest time and effort into the relationship, without expecting immediate results. Sometimes the best connections are built over time, through meaningful interactions, mutual support, and the building of trust.

Trust is a key element in any strategic relationship. Without trust, it is difficult for the relationship to thrive. To build that trust, it is essential to be reliable and demonstrate your commitment. Keeping your promises, being transparent, and acting ethically are fundamental aspects of making people feel that they can count on you. In addition, it is important to be there for people, not only when you need them, but also when they may need your support. Showing interest in their success and being willing to help without expecting anything in return is a powerful way to build strong and lasting relationships.

One of the great benefits of strategic relationships is that they can open doors to new opportunities. These opportunities can come in the form of collaborations, referrals, or even partnerships that you wouldn't have discovered otherwise. When you surround yourself with people who support you and believe in your value, mutually beneficial opportunities are more likely to arise. However, in order for these opportunities to come your way, it's important that you be proactive in maintaining and nurturing those relationships. It's not enough to connect once and then be gone; you must be willing to invest time and energy to grow the relationship.

A key aspect of maintaining strategic relationships is reciprocity. Don't expect to receive without first giving. When you make a conscious effort to help others, they are more likely to want to help you back. Reciprocity doesn't have to be immediate or direct, but it's important that you're always looking for ways to add value to the people you connect with. This can be as simple as sharing an article you think they might be interested in, introducing them to someone in your network who might be helpful, or simply being available to listen and give advice.

Strategic relationships can also be an invaluable source of learning and personal growth. When you surround yourself with people who have different skills, experiences, or perspectives, you have the opportunity to learn from them and broaden your worldview. These relationships challenge you to step out of your comfort zone, see things from different angles, and constantly improve. By building relationships with people who inspire and challenge you, you not only grow professionally, but also personally.

Networking is a useful tool for building strategic relationships, but it's important not to view it as just exchanging business cards or contacts. The real value of networking is in the meaningful connections you can form. Take advantage of events, conferences, or online meetups to meet new people, but don't just stay on the surface level. Ask questions, listen carefully, and look for common ground where you can create a genuine connection. Sometimes, a sincere conversation can take you much further than a simple exchange of contact details.

As you build strategic relationships, it's essential to be patient. The most valuable connections don't always pay off right away. Some of the most important relationships in your professional life can take months or even years to fully develop. That's why it's important not to get discouraged if you don't see immediate results. The key is to continue to build and maintain those relationships over time. Patience and consistency often pay off, sometimes in ways you didn't expect.

In short, building strategic relationships is a vital part of growing your personal brand. It's not just about meeting influencers, but about building genuine connections based on mutual interest, trust, and reciprocity. By surrounding yourself with people who share your values, challenge you to grow, and support you along the way, you'll be creating a powerful network that will help you achieve your goals. Remember that the best relationships are those where both parties benefit and grow together, so focus on adding value and building meaningful connections that last over time.

Positioning yourself as an expert in your field

Positioning yourself as an expert in your field is one of the most effective ways to build a strong, trustworthy personal brand. When people see you as an expert, they are more willing to listen to you, trust what you have to say, and ultimately turn to you for solutions. Becoming an authority figure in a specific area doesn't happen overnight, but it is an achievable process if you commit to continually learning, sharing your knowledge, and consistently demonstrating your expertise.

The first step to positioning yourself as an expert is to identify the specific area in which you want to excel. You may have many skills or interests, but it is essential to choose a specialty in which you truly feel competent and passionate. The more focused you are, the easier it will be for others to recognize you as an expert in that field. Think about what sets you apart from other people in your industry and what you can bring to the table that is unique. It is important that your specialty is aligned with your unique value proposition and reinforces your personal brand image.

Once you have defined your area of expertise, it is time to deepen your knowledge. Knowledge is the foundation on which an expert's reputation is built. This means that you must be willing to constantly learn, stay up to date on the latest trends and developments in your field, and seek to improve your skills. Reading books, attending seminars, taking courses, and keeping an eye on the latest developments will help you consolidate your knowledge and stay relevant. You should never stop learning, because knowledge is not static, and the more you stay up to date, the more value you can offer to others.

However, being an expert doesn't just mean knowing a lot about a topic, it also means sharing that knowledge with others effectively. There's little point in being a great expert if you don't make yourself known. One of the best ways to position yourself as an expert is to share what you know with your audience. You can do this through different channels: writing articles or blog posts, creating content on social media, making videos, or even giving talks and workshops. The important thing is that people see you providing value and that, in doing so, you demonstrate your knowledge in a clear and useful way.

Consistency in content creation is key. If you only share information occasionally, it will be difficult for people to perceive you as an authority. You need to be consistent, both in the quality and quantity of what you share. It's not about overwhelming your audience with information every day, but rather making sure that when you do share something, it's relevant, interesting, and provides value. Consistency is what will allow you to stay top of mind and build that expert image you're looking for.

Another powerful tool to position yourself as an expert is to create a blog or website where you can share your knowledge in a more structured way. A blog allows you to delve deeper into specific topics and offer valuable content that can attract people interested in what you have to say. As you generate more content and position yourself in your niche, people will begin to see you as a reference in that field. Additionally, having your own platform, such as a blog or website, gives you control over how you present your knowledge and helps you build a solid base of followers.

In the digital world, one of the quickest ways to establish yourself as an expert is through social media. Use platforms like LinkedIn, Twitter, or even Instagram or TikTok, depending on where your audience is located, to share your ideas and knowledge. Social media gives you the chance to connect directly with people, answer their questions, and demonstrate your expertise in real time. Plus, it allows you to participate in relevant conversations, which reinforces your presence and positions you as someone who has something valuable to say.

Participating in online debates and discussions can also help you gain visibility as an expert. If there are forums or communities related to your area of expertise, actively engage in them. Answer questions, offer solutions, and share your expertise. Not only does this position you as a reference, but it also helps you build relationships with other influencers in your field. The visibility you can gain by actively participating in these conversations is huge, and every time you provide value, you reinforce your image as an expert.

Collaborations with other experts or influencers in your industry are another effective way to solidify your position. If you have the opportunity to work with someone who is already recognized in your field, whether on projects, interviews, or content collaborations, you will benefit from that person's prestige, which will help strengthen your reputation. When people see you alongside other experts, they are more likely to consider you part of that same circle of authority. Plus, these collaborations allow you to reach new audiences who may not have known you before.

Publishing a book or creating guides and eBooks on your area of expertise can also be a significant step toward positioning yourself as an expert. Writing a book takes time and effort, but if you can offer an in-depth, well-researched resource on a particular topic, you'll establish yourself as an undisputed authority in that field. Even if you don't go so far as to write a full-length book, offering downloadable content, such as free guides or eBooks, can be a great way to demonstrate your knowledge and attract people interested in what you have to offer.

Aside from sharing your knowledge, it is also crucial to demonstrate it in practice. If you have the opportunity to show concrete results from your work or the projects you have been involved in, do not hesitate to do so. People want to see tangible examples of what you can achieve with your expertise. This can be through case studies, testimonials or even by showing your own achievements. By showing that you not only have the theoretical knowledge, but can also apply it effectively, you will strengthen your position as a trusted expert.

Finally, it's important that as you grow as an expert, you stay humble. Being an expert doesn't mean you know everything, or that you can't learn from others. Humility allows you to continue learning and improving, and it also makes you more approachable and trustworthy to your audience. A true expert isn't afraid to admit when they don't know something, and they're always willing to listen and learn from other people. Not only will this attitude help you continue to grow, but it will also allow you to build more authentic and valuable relationships with your audience and other experts in your field.

In short, positioning yourself as an expert in your field takes time, effort, and consistency. You must be willing to continually learn, share your knowledge generously, and build a strong presence on platforms where you can demonstrate your expertise. Over time, people will begin to recognize you as an authority in your area, and your personal brand will be strengthened by the trust you inspire. It's not just about knowing a lot, but knowing how to communicate that knowledge effectively and always staying relevant and accessible.

Lucie Dupont

The Importance of Authenticity and Transparency

Authenticity and transparency are two of the most important pillars for building a strong and lasting personal brand. In a world where information moves at an astonishing speed and where people are constantly exposed to endless messages, the only real way to stand out and build trust is by being authentic and transparent in everything you do. Authenticity is not just about being yourself, but being consistent with your values and beliefs, while transparency involves being honest and open, even when things don't go as you expected. Together, these qualities create a foundation of trust that is key to any personal brand.

Authenticity starts with knowing yourself and being comfortable showing who you are, without the need to pretend to be someone else. When you try to be someone you're not, people notice. While you may think that imitating someone more successful can help you advance faster, the truth is that in the long run, people value originality and genuineness. People are attracted to those who are real, those who aren't afraid to show their imperfections or their vulnerability. You don't need to be perfect to be successful;

what really matters is that you are authentic, that you show up as you are and that you stay true to that.

Being authentic means that your words and actions are aligned. This is especially important when you're building your personal brand, as consistency between what you say and what you do creates a strong, trustworthy image. If you say you value honesty, for example, but your actions show otherwise, people will notice that disconnect and start to doubt you. On the other hand, when you're consistent, people know what to expect from you, which reinforces their trust in your brand. There's nothing more valuable to a personal brand than the trust of your audience, and being authentic is one of the best ways to earn it.

Transparency, on the other hand, goes hand in hand with authenticity. Being transparent means being open and honest, even when things don't go the way you expected or when you make a mistake. We all make mistakes, and there's nothing wrong with admitting it. In fact, being transparent about your failures and the challenges you face can make people respect you even more. Sometimes, when we try to hide our mistakes or gloss over our problems, we risk losing credibility. People value honesty and prefer to deal with someone who is sincere, rather than someone who is always trying to project an image of perfection.

Transparency also means sharing the process behind what you do. Instead of just showing the end results, people are interested in knowing the path you took to get there. This is especially true in the digital world, where audiences are more interested in the "behind the scenes" than the polished perfection that is often shown. By sharing your work process, your challenges, and your learnings, you are opening a window into your world and allowing people to feel more connected to you. This connection is essential to building long-lasting and meaningful relationships with your audience.

Transparency also allows you to manage others' expectations more effectively. If people know what they can realistically expect from you, they're less likely to be disappointed. For example, if you have a deadline for a project and you know you won't be able to meet it, it's best to be transparent from the start. Communicating clearly about any potential delays or problems shows respect for others and reinforces their trust in you. Most people understand that things happen, but what they don't often forgive is miscommunication or dishonesty.

Authenticity and transparency are also essential when it comes to building strategic relationships. The people around you, whether they are collaborators, clients, or followers, want to know that they can trust you. If you are transparent from the beginning about your intentions, your capabilities, and your limits, you will avoid misunderstandings and create an environment of mutual respect. Plus, when you are authentic and transparent, you attract people who value those same qualities, which means that the relationships you build will be based on trust and respect, rather than unrealistic expectations or misunderstandings.

One of the biggest benefits of being authentic and transparent is that it reduces the pressure of trying to be someone you're not. Instead of spending energy on maintaining an image that doesn't truly reflect who you are, you can focus on being the best version of yourself. Not only will this allow you to feel more comfortable in your own skin, but it will also help you attract the right people into your life and business. Those who are drawn to you do so because they value what you truly have to offer, not because you've tried to be someone different.

Additionally, authenticity and transparency are critical to the long-term sustainability of your personal brand. Trends change, fads pass, and the market evolves, but if you build your brand on a solid foundation of authenticity and transparency, you'll always have a competitive advantage. People who trust you will follow you through the changes, because they know they can count on you to be truthful and consistent, regardless of what's going on around you. This is one of the reasons why some personal brands manage to stay strong over time, while others fade away when trends change.

Along the way, you're likely to face situations where being transparent or authentic is a challenge. Maybe you'll face the temptation to hide something or present yourself in a way that doesn't fully align with who you are. In those moments, it's crucial to remember that the trust you've built with your audience is far more valuable than any short-term gains you might gain by being less than honest. Staying true to yourself and your values, even when it's difficult, is what will ultimately solidify your personal brand and allow you to succeed in the long run.

In short, authenticity and transparency are essential ingredients to building a strong, trustworthy, and long-lasting personal brand. By being authentic, you allow yourself to show yourself as you are, which builds deeper, more genuine connections with your audience. By being transparent, you reinforce that trust, showcasing not only your successes, but also your challenges and learnings. Together, these qualities will help you build a reputation that will not only attract the right people, but will also allow you to stay relevant and trustworthy over time. In a world that increasingly values what is genuine and honest, being authentic and transparent is your best bet for success.

Promote your Brand with Strategy

Promoting your personal brand strategically is a crucial part of making your presence visible and relevant in today's world. You can have an amazing personal brand, with a unique value proposition and a compelling story, but if you don't promote it effectively, it's likely not going to achieve the recognition it deserves. Promotion isn't just about talking about yourself, but doing so in a smart, planned way that resonates with the people you want to reach. Promoting your brand strategically means thinking through every action you take to ensure that you're not just making yourself known, but also creating a positive and memorable impact.

The first step in strategically promoting your brand is to define who you want to reach. This is essential because if you don't know who your audience is, it will be very difficult to design a plan that works. You can't speak to everyone at the same time; if you try to do that, you will probably end up not connecting with anyone. You need to be very specific about who your target audience is, what interests they have, what their needs are, and how your brand can help them. By being clear about who you are targeting, you can tailor your message and your way of promoting to be relevant and attractive to those people.

Once you have your audience nailed down, it's time to create an action plan. This is where strategy comes in. Promoting a brand doesn't mean doing everything on the fly or throwing out content without thinking. You need to establish a long-term plan, with clear objectives and concrete steps that will lead you toward those goals. For example, if your goal is to increase brand awareness in a certain sector, you can define specific actions like posting content on social media consistently, collaborating with other experts, or participating in industry events. Each action you take should be aligned with your overall goals, and it's important to measure the results to know what's working and what needs tweaking.

A key aspect of strategic promotion is knowing where and how to appear. Not every platform or medium is suitable for every type of brand, so you need to identify which channels are most effective for you. If, for example, your personal brand is geared towards business professionals,

LinkedIn could be a key platform for you. On the other hand, if your brand is more focused on entertainment or connecting with a younger audience, perhaps Instagram, TikTok or YouTube are better options. The important thing is that you choose the platforms where your audience is already present and where you can create a significant impact. It is better to dominate a few platforms than to try to be on all of them and not have the time or energy to manage them properly.

In addition to choosing the right platforms, it's critical that your content is aligned with the interests and needs of your target audience. It's not enough to just promote for the sake of promoting; you need to create content that actually provides value to your audience. This can be through advice, relevant information, inspiration, or entertainment, depending on what resonates most with the people you're targeting. The more value you offer, the more likely people will be to follow you, trust you, and tell others about you. Remember that the content you share is a fundamental part of your personal brand, and it should reflect your values and unique value proposition.

A common mistake when promoting a personal brand is to focus solely on "me, me, me." While it's important to talk about yourself and what you offer, you also need to balance that focus with a genuine interest in your audience. People don't just want to hear about your accomplishments or how great you are; they want to know how you can help them, what you can bring to them. That's why an effective strategy includes listening to your audience, understanding their problems, and offering solutions. Instead of just talking about yourself, focus on creating a conversation that both you and your audience can benefit from. Not only does this position you as someone who cares about others, but it also strengthens the connection you have with your audience.

Another important part of strategic promotion is consistency. You can't just show up one day and disappear the next, or share content only when you remember. Consistency is key to staying on people's minds and building a long-term relationship with your audience. This means you need to have a well-planned content calendar, making sure you're posting regularly and often enough to keep your audience engaged. It's not about overwhelming your audience with too much information, but rather being consistent in the quality and value of what you share.

In addition to consistency, collaboration is a powerful tool for promoting your personal brand. Collaborating with other people or brands that have a similar audience to yours can help you reach more people faster and more effectively. Collaborations can take many forms, from podcast or video interviews to co-creating content or events. By collaborating with others, you're not only exposing yourself to a new audience, but you're also reinforcing your credibility by partnering with trusted people or brands. It's a great way to leverage networks and grow strategically.

It's also essential to measure the impact of your promotion efforts. A strategy without measurement is like driving without a map; you won't know if you're going in the right direction. Today, there are many tools that allow you to measure how your online promotion is working, such as social media analytics or website metrics. Evaluate what type of content generates the most engagement, which posts attract the most views or comments, and adjust your strategy based on those results. If something isn't working, don't hesitate to change it. Being flexible and adaptable is key to continually improving your approach and maximizing the results of your promotion efforts.

Finally, never underestimate the power of word of mouth. Even though digital marketing and social media are all the talk of the town these days, word of mouth is still one of the most effective forms of promotion. When people speak well of you or recommend your brand to others, it has a huge impact on how others perceive you. That's why part of your promotion strategy should include offering such a positive and valuable experience that your followers or customers are motivated to tell their friends, colleagues or family about you. Every interaction counts, and if you can make people feel good about what you offer, you'll be winning over the best brand advocates.

In short, promoting your personal brand strategically is a process that requires planning, focus, and consistency. It's not just about being present everywhere, but doing it intelligently, in the right places, and with the right message. By clearly defining your audience, creating valuable content, being consistent, and leveraging collaborations, you'll be able to expand the reach of your personal brand and strengthen its presence. Always remember to measure your results and adjust as needed, so that your promotion efforts are effective and lead to long-term success.

Lucie Dupont

Reputation Management and Image Crisis

Managing reputation and image crises is a crucial part of building and maintaining a strong personal brand. Reputation is one of the most valuable assets you have, as it defines how others perceive you, how trustworthy you are, and how they interact with you. However, in the digital world, where opinions are shared quickly and massively, it is easy for a small situation to turn into a crisis that negatively affects your image. The key is knowing how to manage your reputation proactively and being prepared to deal with any image crises that may arise.

The first thing you need to understand about reputation is that it isn't built overnight. It's a constant process that requires time, effort, and consistency. Every interaction, every post, every comment you make affects people's perception of you in some way. That's why it's important to act in a way that's consistent with the values and image you want to project. If you want people to see you as someone trustworthy, for example, you must be honest in everything you do and keep your commitments. If you want to be seen as an authority in your field, you must demonstrate your knowledge and experience through valuable content and actions that support your expertise.

Despite all your efforts to maintain a good reputation, it is inevitable that at some point you will face a difficult situation that puts your image at risk. It could be a misunderstanding, a mistake you made, or even a malicious criticism. The important thing is not so much to avoid these problems altogether, but to know how to handle them effectively when they occur. This is where image crisis management comes into play. Poorly handling a crisis can turn a small situation into a much bigger problem, while good handling can help you emerge stronger from the situation.

When faced with an image crisis, the first step is to stay calm. It's easy to panic when you feel like your reputation is at stake, but reacting impulsively or emotionally can make things worse. Before making any statement or taking any action, it's important to analyze the situation carefully. Ask yourself what's really going on, what's causing the crisis, and how it affects your image. Only when you have a clear understanding of the situation can you act effectively.

Transparency is key during an image crisis. If you made a mistake, the best thing you can do is honestly admit it. People are often understanding when they see someone acknowledges their mistakes and is willing to correct them. Trying to hide or minimize the problem will only create more distrust and make the situation worse. So if you find yourself in a situation where you made a mistake, be transparent from the start. Explain what happened, acknowledge your responsibility, and most importantly, offer a solution. Showing that you are taking steps to fix the situation shows that you are responsible and that you care about your reputation and the people affected.

It's also important to keep in mind that not every criticism or problem requires an immediate public response. Sometimes the best strategy is to listen, assess the situation, and act wisely. Not every criticism is valid or worthy of a response. However, when dealing with an image crisis that can have a significant impact on your reputation, it's critical to act quickly, but always in a thoughtful and strategic manner. Social media and digital media can amplify problems quickly, so it's important not to let a negative situation grow out of control. Responding in a timely and appropriate manner can prevent the crisis from escalating.

Another key aspect of crisis management is communication. In a crisis situation, the way you communicate with your audience can make the difference between calming the situation or inflaming it further. You need to be clear, direct and honest in your communications. Don't try to beat around the bush or use ambiguous language to dodge the issue. People value honesty, and if they feel like you're trying to hide something, their trust in you will be further damaged. Additionally, it's important to be empathetic in your communications. Acknowledging the impact the situation may have had on others and showing that you care about their opinion can help you repair the damage and reconnect with your audience.

A key part of managing an image crisis is learning from it. Every crisis is an opportunity to reflect on what went wrong and how you can improve in the future. Maybe there were warning signs you missed, or maybe the crisis was caused by a mistake that could have been avoided. The important thing is not to ignore the situation once it's over, but to analyze it and take steps to prevent something similar from happening again. This may involve making adjustments to the way you manage your social media, how you communicate with your audience, or the internal processes of your business or personal brand.

In this sense, prevention is the best strategy to avoid image crises from occurring frequently. Maintaining constant and open communication with your audience, acting with integrity, and being alert to any signs of discontent or misunderstanding can help you identify potential problems before they become crises. Additionally, it is helpful to have a crisis action plan prepared in advance, so that when an unexpected situation occurs, you know exactly what to do and do not have to improvise under pressure. A crisis plan can include guidelines on how to communicate, who to involve in resolving the problem, and what steps to take to minimize damage to your reputation.

Finally, it's important to remember that an image crisis, while challenging, doesn't have to mean the end of your reputation. In fact, if you handle the crisis appropriately, you can emerge from it with a stronger reputation than before. People value honesty, responsibility, and the ability to deal with problems with maturity and serenity. If you manage to demonstrate these qualities during a crisis, you're likely to regain the trust of your audience and even gain new followers who appreciate the way you handled the situation.

In short, reputation and image crisis management is a fundamental aspect of a personal brand's success. Maintaining a good reputation requires constant effort and being prepared to face any crisis that may arise. The key is to act with transparency, be honest at all times, communicate clearly and learn from each situation in order to improve in the future. With a solid reputation and crisis management strategy, you will be able to overcome any obstacles that arise and continue building a strong and respected personal brand in the long term.

Lucie Dupont

Evolution of Personal Branding

Personal brand evolution is a natural and necessary process to stay relevant and authentic over time. Just as people change, grow, and adapt, so must your personal brand. It is not static, but dynamic. The brand you start building at one stage of your life or career will not necessarily be the same one you need later on. In fact, a personal brand that does not evolve runs the risk of becoming obsolete or disconnected from new market opportunities and needs.

From the start, it's important to recognize that personal branding isn't a one-time project. It's not just about designing a logo or defining your value proposition once and forgetting about it. A personal brand is like a plant that requires constant care, adaptation to circumstances, and adjustments to stay strong and visible. Just like a plant, if you don't take care to prune it, water it, or relocate it when necessary, it can wilt. In the digital and professional world, trends change quickly, and people's expectations of what you seek to project also evolve. That's why it's vital to be prepared to adjust and evolve over time.

The first step to evolving your personal brand is to always be open to change and learning. People who cling to a fixed image, without adapting to new realities, often get left behind. Part of the evolution process is recognizing that what worked a few years ago may no longer be as effective today. Maybe you started out as an expert in a specific area, but over time you discovered other passions or skills that you also want to integrate into your brand. This doesn't mean you have to abandon what you've already built, but you should look for ways to incorporate those new aspects without losing the essence of what makes you unique.

Self-awareness plays a key role in the evolution of your personal brand. As you progress in your career or personal life, you are faced with new experiences that help you get to know yourself better. What you value, what interests you, and what motivates you can change over time. This internal evolution should be reflected in your brand as well. For example, if at the beginning of your career you focused on a very specific niche, such as technology, but now you have developed an interest in topics related to sustainability, you could adapt your brand to include this new focus. The important thing is that the personal brand you project is aligned with who you are today, not with an old version of yourself.

As your personal brand evolves, it's also crucial to be mindful of how your audience perceives you. People who follow or know you may have expectations about who you are or what you stand for, and it's important to clearly communicate changes to your brand to them to avoid confusion. Transparency in this process is key. If you're transitioning in your career or changing your focus, don't be afraid to share your journey with your audience. Not only does this allow them to stay connected to you, but it can also inspire them to be flexible and open to change in their own lives.

In addition to internal changes, the evolution of personal branding is also influenced by external factors, such as market trends, new technologies, and public demands. If you work in a rapidly changing industry, such as digital marketing or technology, you will likely need to adjust your personal brand frequently to stay relevant. This doesn't mean you should follow every trend, but you should stay informed about what's happening in your industry and adapt when necessary. For example, if a few years ago being active on Facebook was essential for your brand, today it may be more important to have a strong presence on Instagram or LinkedIn, depending on your target audience and career goals.

Another important part of evolving a personal brand is the ability to reinvent yourself. This is especially relevant if you reach a point where you feel like you've reached the limit of what your current brand can offer you. Maybe you've been successful in one area, but you feel like you're ready to explore new horizons or take on new challenges. In these cases, reinventing yourself doesn't mean starting from scratch, but rather taking the foundations you already have and transforming them into something bigger or different. People who successfully reinvent themselves are often those with a greater ability to adapt and a clear vision of where they want to go in the future.

It's important to note that the evolution of a personal brand should not happen abruptly. Radical changes without proper planning can confuse your audience and cause you to lose the connection you've built with them. Instead of making sudden changes, evolution should be a gradual and well-thought-out process. You can start by introducing small variations in the type of content you share, adjusting your message, or exploring new conversation topics that interest you. Over time, these small modifications will help your personal brand transform organically, without generating rejection or confusion among your audience.

Authenticity is another key to successful evolution. Over time, it's important that any changes you make to your personal brand genuinely reflect who you are and where you're going. People value authenticity and can easily tell if you're trying to push an image that isn't consistent with you. This doesn't mean you can't change, but the changes you make should be aligned with your real values, interests, and abilities. If you stay authentic throughout the process, your personal brand evolution will not only be embraced, but appreciated by your audience.

Finally, it's crucial to remember that the evolution of your personal brand is an ongoing process. There is no end point at which you can say your brand is completely finished. There will always be new opportunities, new challenges, and new areas of growth to explore. Flexibility and a willingness to adapt to circumstances are the qualities that will allow you to maintain a strong and relevant personal brand over time. So, rather than seeing the evolution of your brand as a task you need to complete, see it as an ever-developing journey, one in which there is always something new to learn and improve.

In short, personal brand evolution is a natural and necessary process to stay relevant and authentic in an ever-changing world. It involves being open to learning, adjusting your brand based on your own internal changes and external demands, and doing so gradually and authentically. With a flexible attitude and a willingness to reinvent yourself when necessary, you will be able to maintain a strong personal brand that reflects the best of you at every stage of your life and career.

Lucie Dupont

Personal Branding in the Digital World

Personal branding in the digital world has taken on unprecedented importance. Before, building a reputation required time, in-person interactions, and a well-established career in an industry. But today, thanks to social media and other digital platforms, you can start building a personal brand from anywhere in the world and reach thousands, if not millions, of people quickly and effectively. This has opened up endless opportunities for those who want to position themselves as experts, thought leaders, or simply stand out in their field, whatever it may be.

The first thing you need to understand is that in the digital world, all eyes are on you, even when you don't notice it. Everything you post on social media – every comment, photo or video – contributes to people's perception of you. This perception is the foundation of your personal brand. If you're not aware of how you project yourself in the digital realm, you could be giving off an image that doesn't align with who you are or what you want to achieve. That's why it's essential to be intentional about what you share and how you interact in the digital space.

A key advantage of the digital world is that it allows you to have much greater control over your personal brand. Instead of relying on others to speak for you, you can use digital tools to your advantage to tell your own story and shape the narrative you want others to perceive. Social media platforms like Instagram, Twitter, LinkedIn, YouTube, and even personal blogs or websites, offer you platforms to share your vision, your knowledge, and your skills. Through these platforms, you can communicate your message directly, building relationships with your audience and showcasing the unique value you offer.

For example, if you want to position yourself as an expert in personal finance, you can start sharing content that demonstrates your knowledge on the topic. This could include financial advice in the form of tweets, how-to videos on YouTube, or articles on your personal blog. By consistently and genuinely offering value, people will slowly start to see you as an authority in that field. This process is at the heart of how you build a personal brand in the digital world: by offering relevant, valuable content that resonates with your audience.

However, it's important to remember that the digital world also presents challenges. One of the main ones is the amount of noise on these platforms. Millions of posts and content are generated every day, which can make it difficult to stand out. To stand out in this sea of information, it's vital to find your own voice and style. This means being authentic and consistent with what you share. Authenticity is key to generating a real connection with your audience. People can quickly tell if you're being genuine or just trying to appear something you're not.

Another challenge is that in the digital world, everything is recorded. What you post online can stay there indefinitely, and any mistakes or misunderstandings can quickly be amplified. This makes managing your reputation even more critical. You need to be careful about what you share, making sure it's always aligned with the image you want to project. It doesn't mean you can't be spontaneous or relaxed, but it's always helpful to remember that what you say or do online can have a lasting impact on your personal brand.

Consistency plays a key role here. It's not enough to post a couple of times a year or whenever you feel inspired. Personal branding in the digital world requires a constant presence. This doesn't mean you have to be online all the time, but you should maintain a frequency of posting that allows you to stay in your audience's mind on a regular basis. Consistency helps build trust. If people see that you're always there, sharing valuable content, they'll start to associate you with reliability and knowledge.

One aspect that shouldn't be overlooked is interacting with your audience. In the digital world, it's not just about talking, it's also about listening. Responding to comments, participating in discussions, and being attentive to what people think or need are all ways to strengthen your personal brand. Authentic and respectful interactions allow you to build a closer relationship with your community. These relationships are what will often lead to professional opportunities, collaborations, and partnerships that you wouldn't have gotten otherwise.

Digital collaborations are another powerful tool to strengthen your personal brand. Collaborating with other professionals, influencers, or brands that share your values or interests can help you reach new audiences and increase your credibility. These collaborations can be as simple as participating in a joint project, doing online interviews, or making shared posts. The important thing is to make sure that these partnerships are authentic and provide value to both parties.

It's also important to understand that personal branding in the digital world isn't limited to just one platform. While you may prefer to focus on a particular social network or website, diversifying your presence across different platforms can be beneficial. Each network has its own style and type of audience, and tailoring your content to these spaces will allow you to reach a wider audience. For example, LinkedIn is great for establishing yourself as a serious professional and sharing content from your industry, while Instagram can showcase a more creative and visual side of your brand. Exploring different platforms will help you expand your reach and connect with different segments of people.

As your personal brand grows in the digital world, it's also important to monitor your progress and make adjustments when necessary. There are tools and metrics you can use to see how your content is performing, how much engagement you're generating, and what types of posts resonate most with your audience. Staying on top of this data will allow you to adjust your strategy when necessary and focus on what's really working. Don't be afraid to experiment with new types of content or formats, as long as you stay consistent with your overall message and purpose.

Ultimately, the key to building a strong personal brand in the digital world is patience. While it's true that digital platforms allow you to reach a large audience quickly, building a strong personal brand takes time. It's not just about gaining followers or likes, but about building a reputation that is long-lasting and genuine. By investing in authentic relationships, offering constant value, and being consistent in your message, you'll be building a personal brand that will not only open doors for you, but will allow you to stand out in an increasingly competitive digital world.

In short, personal branding in the digital world is a powerful tool that allows you to control your narrative, reach a global audience, and stand out in your field. To do this effectively, you must be intentional about what you share, be authentic, maintain consistency, and be willing to listen and learn from your audience. Although the process can be challenging, the benefits of having a well-positioned personal brand in the digital world are enormous and can open doors to new opportunities and connections.

The Benefits of Having a Healthy Personal Brand

Having a healthy personal brand is like having a solid foundation on which you can build your career, professional relationships, and long-term reputation. When we talk about a "healthy" personal brand, we mean one that is consistent, authentic, and sustainable—one that projects a positive and trustworthy image and genuinely represents you. The benefits of a well-maintained personal brand go far beyond simply having public recognition or more followers on social media; they directly affect your personal and professional success in ways you may not even imagine.

One of the most important benefits of having a healthy personal brand is the trust you generate in others. When people see that you are consistent in what you say and do, and that your message is clear, they tend to trust you more. Trust is one of the most important foundations in any type of relationship, whether professional or personal. If you have a personal brand that people find credible, it will be much easier for them to want to work with you, hire you, or recommend you. Trust generates opportunities because when people believe in you, they feel comfortable supporting you, collaborating with you, or investing in what you offer.

Another great benefit is differentiation in a saturated market. In the world of work, and even more so in the digital environment, competition is fierce. Many people offer services or products similar to yours, but what will make you stand out will not always be your product or your technical skills, but your personal brand. Having a healthy personal brand allows you to stand out because it differentiates you from others. No matter how many people do the same thing as you, if you manage to build an authentic and unique personal brand, there will always be something that makes you special and allows you to stand out. It is your story, your value proposition and how you present yourself that can really make the difference.

Additionally, a healthy personal brand gives you more control over your career. By building a clear and strong image of who you are and what you stand for, you have the ability to steer your career in the direction that interests you most. Instead of waiting for opportunities to come to you, a well-built brand allows you to seek them out and create them. For example, if you position yourself as an expert in a specific field, people are likely to seek you out when they need advice, collaborations, or when opportunities arise in that sector. This puts you in a position of power where you decide which projects to accept and which not to, allowing you to have more control over your career path.

Another key benefit is that a healthy personal brand opens doors for you. Job, collaboration, or growth opportunities tend to come more frequently when you have a strong and consistent public image. If people know who you are, what you stand for, and the quality you offer, they are more likely to seek you out when new opportunities arise. This can include anything from job offers to invitations to speak, participate in projects, or be part of new initiatives. Having a strong brand positions you as someone valuable and desirable to others.

Clarity in your message is also an important benefit. When you have a healthy personal brand, your message is clear and consistent, making it easier for others to quickly understand who you are and what you offer. This clarity is crucial because, in a world where information flows quickly, people often don't have time to dig deep. If your personal brand is well-defined, people can get the gist of you within a few seconds, helping you attract the right people more effectively. A clear message is like a gateway to better opportunities.

A healthy personal brand also builds respect and recognition in your industry. As you position yourself as a trustworthy person with a clear message, others in your field will begin to recognize you as a reference or authoritative voice in what you do. This respect is something that is not earned overnight, but once you have it, it becomes an extremely valuable asset. Being respected in your industry not only brings you immediate benefits, such as more business opportunities or collaborations, but it also helps you stay relevant in the long run.

The consistency of a healthy personal brand is also a great ally in building long-lasting relationships. People tend to gravitate toward those who show up consistently and authentically over time. If you constantly change direction, message, or approach, you're likely to be perceived as unstable or unreliable. But if you stay true to your core and values, the relationships you build will be stronger and longer-lasting. People value stability and consistency, so they'll be more inclined to work with you long-term if they see you as someone who stands firm on their brand.

One of the most valuable aspects of having a healthy personal brand is the personal satisfaction that comes with it. Knowing that you are projecting an image that truly represents you, and that what others see in you is genuine, provides a high degree of personal satisfaction. There is nothing worse than feeling like you have to pretend to be something you are not just to fit in or impress. With a well-built personal brand, you don't have to put on masks or pretend to be someone else. You can feel proud to show the world who you really are, and that brings with it a sense of fulfillment that few manage to achieve.

Additionally, a healthy personal brand helps you build a community around you. As people are drawn to your message, they start following you, supporting you, and sharing your ideas. This community can be comprised of clients, colleagues, mentors, or simply people who admire your work. Having a strong community around you provides you with a support network, opens doors, and helps you amplify your message even further. And the best part is that this community is usually made up of people who truly align with your values and goals, making relationships much more authentic and meaningful.

Work-life balance is another benefit of having a healthy personal brand. When you are authentic in the way you present yourself and maintain consistency between your personal and professional values, it is easier to find a balance between both aspects of your life. You don't have to waste energy trying to be someone different in your work life and your personal life. Instead, you can integrate both harmoniously, allowing you to feel more at peace with yourself and enjoy a more balanced life.

Lastly, a healthy personal brand is also a source of inspiration. When you build a brand that is genuine and authentic, it benefits not only you but those around you as well. People can look to your example and be inspired to follow their own paths, be true to themselves, and build something of their own. Being a source of inspiration is an incredible benefit because it connects you with others in a deeper way and allows you to positively impact their lives. Furthermore, this impact has a multiplier effect, as the people you inspire can also inspire others, creating a network of positive influence that expands beyond you.

In short, the benefits of having a healthy personal brand are immense. From building trust and differentiating yourself in a crowded marketplace, to opening doors, building lasting relationships, and finding a balance between your personal and professional life, a strong personal brand provides you with the tools you need to achieve your goals and stay true to yourself. It's not just about how others perceive you, but also how you feel about yourself knowing that you're projecting an authentic image that's consistent with who you really are.

Taking care of your brand in the long term

Taking care of your personal brand for the long term is essential if you want to maintain a strong and relevant reputation over time. Creating a strong personal brand is just the first step, but what is truly important is how you maintain it and make it evolve over the years. The world is constantly changing, trends, technologies and people's expectations are changing, and if you don't adapt to these changes, your brand can fall behind or even lose value. Taking care of your personal brand means making sure it remains consistent, authentic and aligned with your goals, but also flexible enough to grow and adapt when necessary.

One of the first steps to taking care of your brand for the long term is to stay consistent. Consistency is the key to letting people know what to expect from you, and it's what gives them confidence in what you stand for. This doesn't mean you can never change or evolve, but the essence of your brand needs to stay intact. If you've built your reputation on certain values or skills, it's important to continue to stay true to those principles. For example, if your brand has been focused on authenticity and transparency, people will expect you to remain genuine as time goes on. If you suddenly change course or deviate from those principles, you can create confusion and lose the trust of those who follow you.

However, while consistency is important, so is evolution. Taking care of your brand for the long term doesn't mean staying stagnant. Brands that don't evolve risk becoming obsolete or irrelevant. As the world changes, you must also be willing to adapt your message and presence to new circumstances. The key is to find a balance between maintaining the essence of your brand and allowing it to grow and adjust to new realities. This may mean learning new skills, exploring new communication formats, or even adjusting your value proposition to stay relevant to your audience.

Part of this evolution process involves staying up-to-date and connected to your industry and your audience. The digital world, in particular, changes very quickly, so you need to stay on top of trends, tools, and technologies that can impact the way you communicate and present yourself to the world. This doesn't mean you should follow every fad or try to be on every platform, but you do need to be aware of the changes that are happening and consider how they might affect your brand. Staying up-to-date will allow you to make strategic adjustments when necessary and ensure your brand remains competitive.

Another key aspect of taking care of your personal brand in the long term is maintaining your relationships. The people you interact with, both professionally and personally, play a major role in the perception of your brand. The strategic relationships you build throughout your career can open doors for you, but they can also help you stay relevant. By cultivating these relationships over time, you show that you value people and care about the connections you create. Staying in touch with your network, supporting them in their own projects, and being there when they need you are all ways to strengthen those ties and ensure that you remain visible in their minds.

Taking care of your personal brand also means being aware of how you handle criticism and failure. At some point, we all face difficult situations, mistakes, or criticism, and how you respond to these circumstances is crucial to the perception of your brand. Instead of hiding or trying to ignore problems, it's important to face them with transparency and honesty. If you make a mistake, admitting it and learning from the situation can strengthen your brand rather than weaken it. How you handle adversity shows your character, and people value those who are responsible and able to face challenges with integrity.

Authenticity is another essential component to taking care of your personal brand for the long term. In a world where information spreads quickly and where people are looking for real connections, being authentic is more important than ever. Authenticity isn't something you can fake or manufacture—it must come from who you really are. This means being honest about your strengths and weaknesses, being transparent in your interactions, and staying true to your values. People are very perceptive and can tell if you're trying to be something you're not, which can seriously damage your brand. Maintaining your authenticity over time will help your brand be seen as genuine and trustworthy.

Another key aspect of taking care of your personal brand is having a long-term approach. Many people focus only on immediate success or getting quick results, but if you want to build a brand that lasts, you need to think beyond the immediate. This means making decisions that will benefit your brand over time, even if they may not yield instant results. For example, investing in relationships, creating valuable content, or constantly improving your skills are actions that may not show immediate results, but that will, over time, strengthen your personal brand significantly.

Furthermore, adaptability is a core value. The world changes rapidly, and the ability to adapt to new environments, technologies, and situations is vital to your brand's long-term success. This doesn't mean changing who you are, but rather being flexible in how you present yourself and how you apply your skills in different contexts. If you're adaptable, you'll be better able to respond to market changes, take advantage of new opportunities, and stay relevant in your field. Adaptability also allows you to innovate and try new things without losing sight of the essence of what makes you unique.

Taking care of your brand in the long term also requires a strategic approach to your online presence. The digital footprint you leave online is an important part of your brand, and it's something that remains even after posts or interactions have been forgotten. That's why it's crucial to be careful about what you share, make sure your social media profiles are up to date, and maintain a professional presence at all times. Additionally, constantly monitoring your online reputation will allow you to quickly identify any issues or misunderstandings and correct them before they become a bigger problem.

Finally, it's important to keep a focus on personal and professional growth. Taking care of your personal brand isn't just about maintaining the image you already have, but also about continuing to improve, learn, and grow. This means being willing to invest in your education, whether through courses, books, or experiences that allow you to acquire new skills and knowledge. The more you grow as a person and as a professional, the more value you can bring to your brand and those around you. Continued growth will allow you to keep your brand fresh and relevant over time.

In short, nurturing your personal brand for the long term requires a careful and conscious approach. Staying consistent but open to evolution, building and maintaining strong relationships, handling criticism appropriately, being authentic and adaptable, and having a growth mindset are all key aspects of ensuring your brand not only stays strong, but continues to grow and evolve over time. It's an ongoing effort, but one that will reward you with a strong reputation, long-lasting relationships, and opportunities that will continue to appear throughout your career.

www.ingramcontent.com/pod-product-compliance
Lightning Source LLC
Chambersburg PA
CBHW021956170726
47994CB00021B/816